How to Define and Build an Effective Cyber Threat Intelligence Capability

How to Define and Build an Effective Cyber Threat Intelligence Capability

Henry Dalziel

AMSTERDAM • BOSTON • HEIDELBERG
LONDON • NEW YORK • OXFORD • PARIS
SAN DIEGO • SAN FRANCISCO
SINGAPORE • SYDNEY • TOKYO

Syngress is an Imprint of Elsevier

Syngress is an imprint of Elsevier
225 Wyman Street, Waltham, MA 02451, USA

Notices
Knowledge and best practice in this field are constantly changing. As new research and experience broaden our understanding, changes in research methods or professional practices, may become necessary. Practitioners and researchers must always rely on their own experience and knowledge in evaluating and using any information or methods described here in. In using such information or methods they should be mindful of their own safety and the safety of others, including parties for whom they have a professional responsibility.

To the fullest extent of the law, neither the Publisher nor the authors, contributors, or editors, assume any liability for any injury and/or damage to persons or property as a matter of products liability, negligence or otherwise, or from any use or operation of any methods, products, instructions, or ideas contained in the material herein.

British Library Cataloguing-in-Publication Data
A catalogue record for this book is available from the British Library.

Library of Congress Cataloging-in-Publication Data
A catalog record for this book is available from the Library of Congress.

ISBN: 978-0-12-802730-1

For information on all Syngress publications
visit our website at http://store.elsevier.com/

Working together
to grow libraries in
developing countries

www.elsevier.com • www.bookaid.org

TABLE OF CONTENTS

AUTHOR BIOGRAPHY

Henry Dalziel is a serial education entrepreneur, founder of Concise Ac Ltd, online cybersecurity blogger, and e-book author. He writes for the blog "Concise-Courses.com" and has developed numerous cybersecurity continuing education courses and books. Concise Ac Ltd develops and distributes continuing education content (books and courses) for cybersecurity professionals seeking skill enhancement and career advancement. The company was recently accepted onto the UK Trade & Investment's (UKTI) Global Entrepreneur Programme (GEP).

CONTRIBUTING EDITORS' BIOGRAPHY

Eric Olson is Vice President, Product Strategy at Cyveillance, where he is responsible for the management of Cyveillance's entire portfolio of Enterprise and OEM services. He oversees new product development, messaging and positioning, pricing strategy, and profitability for each service line.

James Carnall is Vice President, Cyber Intelligence Division at Cyveillance, where he is responsible for Brand Protection, Cyber Security, and Anti-Phishing services. James also manages the Cyber Intelligence Analyst Team, as well as the Global Intelligence and Legal Advisory Teams.

CHAPTER *1*

Introduction

One of the most important concepts in the world of information security today is defining and building an effective Cyber Threat Intelligence capability. To ensure that all the concepts are covered, we have teamed up with Cyveillance, a world leader in cyber intelligence, to create a storyline that covers the following topics.

We start with discussing why the notion of defining an effective capability is so important. As we will see, threat intelligence is one of the buzzwords of the day, but it means different things to different people. As a result, it can end up meaning next to nothing, unless you define it according to your organization's individual goals.

As a cybersecurity professional, you may have been exposed to the current trend to discuss, plan, or even build and operate some kind of cyber threat center, "super SEIM," super SOC or whatever your particular organization may have chosen to call it. Despite a lot of buzz, startup money, and industry discussion, what we have seen most often is that there are *far* more organizations in the "planning" stage, the "thinking about it" stage or the "wondering if it's a good idea" stage than those successfully operating a functional center, and it is for that larger group, that is, those who are not yet in operation, or are just getting started, for whom this book is intended.

There's a lot of technical jargon thrown around, but in our opinion, it really boils down to the following: Why, What, How and Who. Each of those elements will be tackled in detail in the following chapters. You will also be introduced to an easy-to-follow process to translate your objectives – or the "why" in colloquial terms – into activities and needs, or the "what." With this information at hand, you will be able to determine what intelligence you would need on the basis of those objectives, that is, the options available to you to build a program, and how the process can be implemented to make your center or threat intelligence capability a reality.

Another key aspect we cover is an overview of the common landmines that organizations tend to step on. This book will go over the keys to successful implementation, which is really a nice way of saying how to avoid stepping on those landmines! Then, and only then would it be worth discussing who the right vendors, partners, or employees are to build, staff, and run your cyber threat intelligence program.

Last, but not by any means the least, the book will cover reporting and management communication as well as its importance in an effective threat intelligence operation. From there, the conversation will come to an end at the "block and tackle" planning, budgeting, and submitting a request for money stage, without which none of this happens.

Before getting down to the nitty-gritty of cyber threat intelligence, we would like to share a quote. Taken from Lewis Carroll's Alice in Wonderland, it is part of a conversation between Alice and the Cheshire Cat, but it is also applicable in real life while talking to stakeholders in the planning or thinking stages of building a threat intelligence capability.

> Alice: Would you tell me please, which way I ought to go?
> The Cat: Well that depends a good deal on where you want to get to.
> Alice: I don't care much where.
> The Cat: Then it doesn't matter which way you go, does it?

Any threat intelligence program that does not support a clear business objective; pursue a well-defined mission that is bounded, scoped and relatively rigid; work within a set of clear expectations in a portfolio of responsibilities that everyone agrees to; and meaningfully report metrics that matter to management and budget holders is doomed, in our opinion, to fail.

These factors are critical to understand at the outset for defining and building a threat intelligence capability. If you do not ensure that these elements are considered, if you do not set out with a clear end state in mind, you are like Alice talking to the Cheshire Cat. If you do not know where you are going, it is easy to meander about, spending time and money, with no clear idea of where you are going, or knowing if you are actually getting any closer to your destination.

A Problem Well-Defined is Half-Solved

Threat intelligence is absolutely the buzzword "du jour." It is being used to seek venture capital and fund start-ups. It is being aggressively pitched to the enterprise market by the provider industry as the solution to all their woes. Well, to put a fairly aggressive stake in the ground, we would argue that the majority of what is being sold and billed as "threat intelligence" is not. It is data. From lists of bad IPs, or application vulnerabilities, or malware signatures, or URL blacklists, to botted nodes, or botnet C2 servers, or social media data; from open source or web-based content to RSS feeds and IRC channels, in their initial form, *none* of these things is "intelligence," they are data.

2.1 DATA FEEDS VS. INTELLIGENCE

Our contributing editor, Cyveillance, will tell you they love data. Data is great! They produce data, buy data, sell data, and there is no question data plays a pivotal role here. However, we are going to cover the subject of data as it relates specifically to building a threat intelligence capability, and there is an absolute distinction between data and intelligence. So, in the spirit of "a problem well-defined is half-solved," we can save a lot of confusion if we start by explicitly defining the differences between data and intelligence to truly understand the issue.

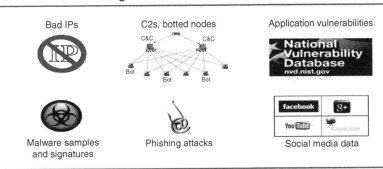

Most "threat intelligence"... are not

Bad IPs   C2s, botted nodes   Application vulnerabilities

Malware samples and signatures   Phishing attacks   Social media data

Data, (the stuff so often marketed as "intelligence") is typically some form of machine-readable feed, file, or service in a format like XML, JSON, or CSV, or an API, web service, or some other access point for information that go from one machine to another machine to be read by a machine. There are lots of feeds and services like this out there, and many of them are actually extremely useful, but to be explicit, anyone selling you a feed of this would be selling you a *data* feed, not an *intelligence* feed. Well, if we have now said what intelligence *is not*, let us explicitly state what we believe it *is*.

2.2 DEFINING THREAT INTELLIGENCE

From a professional's perspective, intelligence is data that has been put through a logical and analytical process, most often a human-based process that evaluates the data in context and produces a usable output. In rare cases, there are options for that process to be entirely machine driven if the outcome allows an action, change in security or defensive posture, or decision that was not possible before the process. In any event, whether the data is transformed or distilled or otherwise turned into usable intelligence by software or neurons, the output must meet at least the following three requirements to meet the definition of intelligence. The information must be:

Defining threat intelligence

Intelligence is data that has been refined, analyzed, or processed such that it is *relevant, actionable,* and *valuable.*

1. *Relevant:* The information must relate to, or at least potentially relate to, *your* enterprise, industry, networks, and/or objectives.

2. *Actionable:* It must be specific enough to prompt some response, change, action, or decision, or to inform an explicit decision *not* to act.

3. *Valuable:* Even if relevant and actionable, if the data (and the action) do not contribute to any useful business outcome, there is no value.

⊕ Cyveillance

1. *Relevant*: It must be relevant to your enterprise/ industry/ business objectives, or some other aspect of organizational life. Take for instance

a company that runs Linux for all its servers, and all its desktop are Apple Macs. Now a vendor comes to them saying, "Hi, I am a sales person for XYZ Co. I have vulnerability threat intelligence." About 98% of the data this vendor may be delivering focuses on vulnerabilities in Microsoft Windows or Windows applications. It may actually be great data, but it is in no way *relevant* to an enterprise that does not run a single Windows machine.

Although this example seems quite simplistic, it is just a way to illustrate the following point: data must be relevant to the organization or it can be the world's greatest and/or most interesting data for the sake of intellectual exercise. However, if it does not impact the organization and is not relevant to it, it cannot be threat intelligence applied to that organization.

2. *Actionable*: The data must be actionable, a term you are probably familiar with since everyone, including vendors, likes to use it. It is in fact a little bit of a misnomer; but the misnomer takes too long to fit on a marketing slick. To ensure full clarity, the concept of actionable means that it must be specific enough to do one of two things:

- It must either prompt, enable, or inform some response, action, decision, or change in security posture, configuration, level of sensitivity or other organizational network or human change to the environment; OR
- It must provide sufficient information to support making an *informed* decision not to act. That is, not acting is in fact an action, so long as it is an informed choice not to act that is made out of considered evaluation, rather than just inaction out of ignorance.

To illustrate this point, here is an example. Imagine establishing context, specifics, and a risk assessment around an event. For example, suppose an attempted penetration of a network or attempted spear phishing of an employee occurs. Now you may discern on the basis of your investigation or review that the hacker is unsophisticated, that the attack does not actually pose a threat or reflect any kind of serious activity targeting the organization, and the attempt was crude and easily neutralized. Although a more sophisticated attempt might prompt increased authentication requirements, data egress rule changes, employee training or some other response, in this case your evaluation might support an *informed* decision to take none of those steps due to the low level of risk posed by the unsophisticated attack. In this case, no action still falls under the definition of actionable intelligence because the "not taking action" was an informed decision.

3. *Valuable*: The information must be valuable, and at the organization (not department) level, value must translate to the *business*. Security professionals, although often experts in their fields, often lack the vocabulary, business background, or skills to understand and make this argument. Even if the data or information is relevant, actionable, and capable of allowing the security team to do something that they believe is in the organization's interest from a security perspective, the organization will be robbed of value if its security experts cannot translate or align their operational activities of a threat center, a threat intelligence function or similar team with the business objectives of the company. Regardless of whatever your cyber center, fusion center, and so forth may be called within your company, the threat intelligence function may not get off the ground or may be short lived if the experts cannot align and report their activities with the aim to achieve some useful business outcome that ensures both start-up and on-going funding and support. Therefore, it is vital that you know how to translate the value back to the business.

CHAPTER 3

Defining Business Objectives
or "Start with Why"

Defining Business Objectives, "Start with Why"

At a macro level, there are only a few business imperatives that justify the work, effort, and expenditure for doing *anything*. The objective = the WHY

| Revenue or margin Customer Sat. and retention Employee Sat. and retention | Expenses risk | Because you have to |

 Cyveillance

As mentioned earlier, most of the chapters in this book leverage a simple construct or sequence of "Why, What, How and Who". In this case, when it comes to why start, build, plan or even have a conversation about planning or building a threat intelligence capability, it is important to start with "why" at a business level. If you belong to the nonprofit or governmental sectors, the term business objectives may not apply. You can, however, translate that to organizational objectives or agency mission. In other words, if you are part of a military unit, a nonprofit or a civilian agency, some of the "why's" may be a little different than what you read here. For a commercial organization, though, there are really only six macro-level reasons to do anything.

1. Growing revenue, or the margin on the revenue you have already have
2. Lowering expenses
3. Reducing business risk
4. Increasing customer satisfaction and retention, which eventually should translate to more revenue or more margin, but which are worthwhile objectives in their own right

5. Increasing employee retention and satisfaction, which eventually should translate to lower expenses, but which are again worthwhile objectives in their own right
6. Complying with regulations or over governmental mandate, that is, "because you just have to"

At the executive management, top floor, corner office level, these are the only six reasons to organizationally bother with the effort, expenditure, and disruption of doing *anything*, especially something new. That has to be the "why" with which defining and building a threat intelligence capability must align.

3.1 WHEN DEFINING BUSINESS OBJECTIVES, LANGUAGE MATTERS

Language matters. The translation from security or intelligence to a perspective that matters to management is a critical step in both the planning and ongoing operations process, and one where security and intelligence professionals sometimes hit some stumbling blocks because they do not have the "interpreter" with the language skills to make that jump. Teams will sometimes employ a dozen very smart people who read raw source code and speak binary, but none who speak "management". Although some do not believe in its power, the translation is going to be very important in both directions.

The words that you choose as a security or risk professional to translate the threat intelligence initiative or request funds for ongoing operations to the management level must be according to the language of the business or organizational mission. It is vital to understand how you can align the threat intelligence group, department, or center's mission with that of the organization and communicate the budget requests, required resources and so forth in the language that management speaks, rather than in the language security professionals speak.

Any organization large enough to be looking at a dedicated intelligence capability – whether through supporting vendors, in-house staff and resources, some hybrid model between the two – should be able to translate that back to the organization's objectives because that is the best, indeed the only way, to ensure the support and resources you will need. Put simply, nothing happens without money. As blunt as that may sound, it is the truth. If you cannot tell the folks with the money why they should give it to you in words and objectives that matter to them (not what matters to you), your effort is likely to be short lived at best.

So before you buy one bit of data, one tool, one data feed or even let a vendor into your office to consider their offerings, sit down and talk with your team. In the case of Cyveillance, they offer a simple checklist. Before reviewing or spending anything, it is important to ask a number of questions internally, and investigating these more deeply will constitute the bulk of this book. But for now, let us set the stage at a high level.

So before you buy (or do not buy) one bit of data...

Before reviewing a single tool or feed or talking to a single vendor, can you answer these high-level questions before you proceed?

1. What is the business driver to buy or build "threat intel" capabilities? Compliance? Risk Reduction? Someone just got back from RSA?

2. Can you define a clear, *and bounded*, mission or set of responsibilities?

3. Can you quantify the problem, the risk or the value of the solution?

4. How will you operationalize the information to support business goals?

5. How will you report and measure performance to justify expenditures?

If you cannot effectively answer these questions, <u>STOP</u>. **Cyveillance**
a Qinetiq Company

© Cyveillance, Inc. 2014   Cyveillance Confidential

Once you have your WHY...

Tools, data, and finished intelligence are all potential tools in enhancing the security of your data, employees, network, and enterprise, *so long as*:

1. You know **WHY**: A clear business objective and defined mission will be key to both budget justification and successful implementation.

2. WHY defines **WHAT**: The business objective dictates the scope of the mission and what types of threat intelligence you will need.

3. You also need to know **HOW**: An implementation model must turn data into something useful or the project *cannot* succeed.

4. Once you know why you are doing it, what you will need and how you will use it, *then* you can evaluate **WHO** and where to buy.

Cyveillance
a Qinetiq Company

© Cyveillance, Inc. 2014   Cyveillance Confidential

First: What business driver are we in alignment with to buy or build some kind of threat intelligence capability? Are we doing this to meet a compliance requirement? For example, if you are in the financial services industry, you will need to address the recent FFIEC guidelines that were finalized around social media and online monitoring. That is a perfectly valid reason to say, I am going to go out and get some "intelligence" around what is being said online. I have a regulatory requirement and that could be part of the mission of my cyber center. Is it to reduce risk, to be aware of other things that will help you prevent a data breach, things that will help me respond to or discover if a breach has already happened? All laudable goals so long as you can align them explicitly to reducing risk, reducing expenses, or other managerial priorities.

Now there are people who may have other motives. For instance, some people have contracted professionals for the task of building out this capability or pricing out an initial budget request because an executive heard the words "threat intelligence" hundreds of times at a big conference and just realized that it is actually a "thing". Although this is in no way a good reason to look at threat intelligence, it is one that threat intelligence experts are bound to come across.

Another important question is: Will you be able to define a clear and bounded set of mission responsibilities in support of that business objective? This is important because, in large organizations, word will quickly spread that there is a team of "cyber experts" being stood up. The day this happens, you may find everyone from attorneys with their trademark and brand issues, to the compliance officer to the marketing department running to see if they can offload some of their work on you under the rubric of "monitoring the Internet" or "online intelligence." The minute that folks hear that such a structure is underway, they will eagerly seek to hand over some of their work, and let you spend your people and budget doing something they have been doing (or not doing).

This is why a bounded set of responsibilities as well as a portfolio of activities in alignment with that business driver is important. Although your team may well wish to be of help to the counsel's office on domain name issues or marketing on "buzz metrics" or the compliance group on watching for employees blabbing about confidential deals on their Facebook page, if those activities are not in support of the bounded scope and mission that your team can point to as components of their priority list, they will easily become overwhelmed or distracted. Applying the limited capacity to the right activities will be a key to success.

Equally important is this: Can you quantify the problem, the risk or at least the value of solving the problem in any way? Suppose, for example, one year into your intelligence program, nothing bad or scary has happened. Is that because luck was on your side? Or is there any indication that your efforts contributed to that positive outcome? Metrics that are meaningful for reporting and measuring contribution will be very helpful as you progress.

Next, do you have some kind of operational model or architecture that will allow you to ingest, generate, produce, purchase or otherwise beg, borrow or steal the information that becomes intelligence in support of those business goals? What is that operational model? In other words, if you had your people and your budget in place tomorrow and were all set to start building your threat center, do you yet have any idea how you will implement the process? In simple terms, will you plug this data or that cable into that box over there and put it in front of this person in order to make something useful happen? If you do not yet know the implementation or infrastructure approach, it is probably too early to discuss many types of vendors and services. Note that you will also urgently need the participation and support of your IT, networking, or other operations type departments. Many a threat center has been delayed or derailed the moment a plan or design lands in IT and someone says "you are not putting that on *my* network."

And, finally, if all of that infrastructure was actually running today, how would you report and measure performance to justify both the initial and ongoing running costs of doing this? What would you share with management each week or month or quarter to demonstrate not just activity but also value and benefit. Activity for its own sake without business value is called "an opportunity to cut costs next year."

To sum up then, if you cannot answer these five questions, at least preliminarily, *stop*. You are not ready to buy anything, except perhaps some consulting or professional services to help you answer them before you proceed.

1. What is the driver to buy or build threat intelligence capabilities? Compliance? Risk reduction? Someone just got back from RSA?
2. Can you define a clear, and bounded, mission or set of responsibilities?
3. Can you quantify the problem, the risk, or the value of the solution?
4. How will you operationalize the information to support the objective?
5. How will you report and measure performance to justify expenditures?

For many organizations, there actually is a justification to do a great deal of work and investment around threat intelligence; but in order to proceed intelligently and effectively from a business standpoint, you should at least begin to sketch out answers to these questions. How to do that will be covered in the upcoming chapters.

Common Objectives of a Threat Intelligence Program

So we have spoken very conceptually so far. But perhaps you are wondering, "what are a common set of 'why's' in a real-world implementation?" As you know by now, they can be raising or lowering revenue, profit, satisfaction, expense, or risk or ensuring compliance with some kind of requirement or regulation. So how does that translate into actual mission activities?

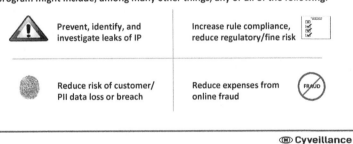

Common objectives of a threat intelligence program

What intelligence do you actually need? Common objectives of a threat intelligence program might include, among many other things, any or all of the following:

Prevent, identify, and investigate leaks of IP

Increase rule compliance, reduce regulatory/fine risk

Reduce risk of customer/ PII data loss or breach

Reduce expenses from online fraud

⟨⊕⟩ **Cyveillance**

© Cyveillance, Inc. 2014   Cyveillance Confidential

Here are a few common examples that come up time and again when experts talk to their customers.

1. Prevent, identify, and investigate leaks of intellectual property or other internal data. This can be customer data, credit-card data, Personal Identity Information (PII), blueprints, schematics, or the company's crown jewel, say, a new holographic smartphone. Whatever the intellectual value, the digital assets within the perimeter are supposed to stay there. Stop them from getting out; figure out where they have already gotten out. If the latter is true, investigate what is out and how it happened.

2. Reduce the risk of consumer PII loss or other customer-data breach. This is not necessarily from inside as in the case of intellectual property. It may be because of supply chains, your ecosystem, your vendor, partner, or provider. Take for instance the massive breach at Target; according to published reports, the attack was believed to have started with the social engineering of an HVAC subcontractor. Your intellectual property and customer data are always at risk, and not necessarily from just within your own network perimeter.
3. Increase compliance or reduce the risk of noncompliance, a regulatory sanction, fine, or other potential consequence of your employees, contractors, partners, or suppliers not doing what they are supposed to do.
4. Reduce expenses incurred by online fraud or other cybercrime activity.

4.1 ONCE YOU HAVE YOUR WHY...

Once you have a "why," that is, a business objective and a defined mission, you will be able to define what kind of intelligence you need to support it. You cannot define what kind of intelligence or data you want to input, ingest, receive, purchase, output, or deliver to management or constituents if you do not know why you are doing it. In other words, the "why" defines the "what."

Once you know what you want to do, and what kind of mission activities you need to support, you can look at how you would implement it. This means that you can choose to build it in-house, outsource it from a vendor, staff it internally or via contractors, or "plug this into that". You cannot determine which of these to go for until you know what it is you are trying to accomplish and why you are doing it. Once you know, you can pick an implementation that would work, for example, a cloud-based model, internal model, fusion center, data feeds, and so forth. Whatever it is, once you know how you are going to implement it, you know how to prequalify anyone who is trying to help, support or sell it to you. Put simply, you proceed from WHY to WHAT to HOW to WHO. The process almost always has to go in that order, and for that reason this is the framework, and sequence used throughout the rest of this book.

CHAPTER 5

Translating Objectives into Needs, or "Why Drives What"

Before reading any further, we should delve down into making a subtle but important distinction: The objectives that you have defined, or the business need you are trying to meet, are not the same as a mission activity.

Your *objective* is not to effectively patch vulnerabilities or defend against DDoS attacks or stop hackers from getting into your network. These are NOT business objectives. They are activities that support a business objective. The business objective might be, "mitigating the risk of increased costs or competitive damage that might ensue from data loss". Those business impacts might include mitigation costs, higher customer-service call volumes, reputational damage, the CEO losing his/her job, or other calamity. If this is the business objective, then activities that support that objective should directly align with them. Just understand there is a distinction between the objective and the activities that support it.

Let us take another simple example. Suppose you define a business objective, for example, "ensure our agents do not make improper statements on their insurance agency web sites and cause a huge fine against our broker-dealer." With that objective clearly stated, you can then define mission activities that support it.

We have chosen a compliance example here by the way, to help illustrate that "risk" is not always necessarily a "threat." Threat should be, and often is, viewed as a subset of risk, and these concepts can blur, especially in finance organizations, pharmaceuticals, and other highly regulated industries. Compliance and regulatory risks may be as important as those tied to malicious activity, and you may very well find addressing these risks is included as part of your group mission. So, to return to our example, if your *objective* is to mitigate compliance risk, then a mission-supporting *activity* might very well be monitoring your independent representatives and agents to ensure that they do not say things or make promises that violate the rules related to selling registered products such as annuities or other financial instruments.

Here is another concrete example. Suppose your *objective* is to minimize the risk of a data breach by an outside threat actor, because breaches raise expenses and damage reputation, brand equity and customer trust, which in turn can reduce revenues. That is the business issue. In this case then, some aligned mission activities might include:

- Ensuring effective prioritization and management of vulnerabilities to reduce risk of infection and data exfiltration;
- Tagging of sensitive data and implementation of a data loss prevention (DLP) or monitoring system to track movement of tagged sensitive data; and
- Cyber-safety awareness training for employees to mitigate spear phishing and social engineering of those with access to the sensitive data or systems.

Once you know your mission activities, they will in turn help you define your intelligence needs. To continue:

- IF the business objective is minimizing the risk of a data breach; AND
- A supporting mission activity is making sure that your employees do not get spear phished, THEN
- One example of an *intelligence need* to support the activity would be a feed, or content that educates the relevant parties about the latest spear phishing attacks and related techniques and practices.

This is a simple example to be sure, but it is meant to show the sequential linkage from objective to activity to intelligence need. Why you are doing something, and what thing you are doing, will in turn define the type of information you need to develop or procure to produce usable, relevant intelligence. That is why it is imperative to start with "why" in order to then define "what."

5.1 ILLUSTRATION: TRANSLATING THE OBJECTIVE INTO CONCRETE INTELLIGENCE NEEDS

Let us continue with concrete, tangible cases to make this as real as possible. For each of the examples above, if the objective is to prevent, identify, and investigate losses of sensitive internal data or intellectual property, then what are the actual mission activities carried out by the group of people who will sit in a room and do the actual work? And how does that list of activities translate into the actual intelligence needs (i.e., the "what" you need to develop or go out and buy)?

One activity might include understanding hacker and threat actor "TTPs" or tactics, techniques and procedures. How are they attacking other organizations? How did that recent breach in the news happen? How did they get into that organization? Who was responsible and what kinds of things do they commonly use to accomplish their goals? If gaining that knowledge is the required activity, then your intelligence need might be defined as a feed, content stream, education program, or other on-going service that educates your team about those threat actors and their TTPs.

Here is another aspect that might tie to this example. Suppose an activity that supports your mission is attempting to detect when data exfiltration is under way, or that a host on your network has been compromised. If that is a key activity, then what types of data could you use to support it so that you can in turn, generate intelligence? (You may recall that what many people sell as intelligence, by our definition, is not. But it may be the data you can turn into intelligence.) A vendor might offer a feed of IP addresses and domain names for current drop sites to which exfiltrated data is being transmitted. By taking that list of IPs and putting it into your infrastructure to prevent or monitor data egress, you now have something that can be applied to your organization, has potential business value, and produces an action or response. Thus, data from the vendor can actually become intelligence.

Another related activity you might define to support this mission is to detect or discover when sensitive data has already left the organization. One activity in support of this would be to scour the internet for internally sourced, or authored data, or documents, focusing in part on some of the sites and markets that are known to deal in such data, for example, PasteBin, Pastey, Pirate Pad, and the likes, hacker Internet Relay Chat (IRC) channels, and forums, document sharing sites like Scribed, Docstock, and Slideshare, or "leak" sites like OpenLeaks, Wikileaks. In this scenario, then, the *activity* is to monitor or check such sources for your own internal materials, and the *data or intelligence need* might be defined as a feed or service that automates or supports you by doing such searching or monitoring, gathering, screening, and delivering to you any sensitive materials that appear in these forums.

So to summarize, if, for example, the objective is to prevent or identify the loss of IP, and the activity is to scour the internet for evidence of IP that has already left the building, then your information needs might include social media or web-based data that indicates things that have left the building, or IPs, indicators-of-compromise (IOCs), or similar technical data that shows it is trying to do so. This is the brass tacks translating high-level business needs all the way down to the activities the group will actually undertake on a day-to-day basis, and the types of intelligence you need to go out and procure or develop internally to fulfill your mission.

How Technology Models Operationalize Threat Data

After going over the "why" aspect, you were also introduced to a business' objective to drive a "what" – which is a set of mission activities, and the intelligence or data needs you should have to support activities where the data is sourced internally, externally, or both. In other words, we are now through "why" and "what." Now, you are much better positioned to look at how to turn all of this information into operational intelligence from the data.

HOW: Technology models to operationalize threat data

Feeds and intelligence can integrate with the enterprise in many ways and places. Which of them applies to you *depends on your answers to the question of WHY.*

Firewalls and gateways · Searchable indices

SIEMs and analytics tools · Visualization and dashboards

(⊕) **Cyveillance**

There are lots of ways organizations are trying to turn information into actionable intelligence, or mold it into tools people can actually use. You can ingest data feeds into firewalls, gateways, or other appliances of various types. You can ingest text data into a searchable index. You can look at packages to normalize, visualize, and store lots of data. As of this writing, there are many options to do *some* of what is needed, but in nearly all cases we have seen, the "solution" has been cobbled together from a range of off-the-shelf and custom parts.

One reason solutions are still largely "home brewed" is the volume and company-specific peculiarities of the data. To handle the so-called "big data", companies evaluate technologies like Hadoop, SOLR, Elasticsearch, MongoDB, or whatever their choice of database for unstructured, semi-structured, and messy data may be. They study visualization and analytics tools from the free open-source libraries like Arbor to extremely powerful, and costly, commercial packages such as Spunk, i2, and Palantir. Some folks refer to the systems that result as "Frankenstein Boxes" since they often began life as a standard off-the-shelf product until the security and IT teams began bolting things onto their sides to try creating a more comprehensive system that actually does all the things its creators need it to do. What seems to be the clear wish is the ability to ingest and normalize internally sourced data such as network traffic, SIM information, log analysis, DLP alerts, etc. that are within the control of the staff and inside the perimeter, with external data such as feeds from intelligence providers, including human-readable written product and machine-readable data in formats such as STIX, XML, and JSON.

This book does not and will not advocate for one method or product over another. In fact, in a moment, you will see very much the opposite. What we can say at this point is that, if (as of this writing) there is an available product that does the type of intelligence support and correlation just described, the authors are unaware of it, and many companies are desperately seeking it. Regardless, whether you could buy such a solution, or have to build one out yourself, it is important to understand that before you go out and start buying things, there needs to be an architectural plan for how you are going to support those mission activities and the type of intelligence you just decided you need.

6.1 HOW- LABOR OPTIONS OR "HOW MUCH DO I DO MYSELF?"

In addition to technological implementation options, there is also the question of who is going to do the work. Some of the largest organizations that enjoy substantial budgets and executives buy-in on the importance of threat intelligence, can dare to look at one extreme end of the spectrum: build everything they need themselves.

If your company fits this description, you can task or hire a whole bunch of people to select technologies, cobble them together, build the Frankenstein box, and then bring in a completely different group of people to run it, since it is rare for both coders and engineers to be experienced threat analysts and investigators. Some people will go for the absolute build method that entails cobbling together the technology, selecting all the vendors, ingesting all the data, normalizing it all, visualizing it, putting the analysts and investigators in front of it, and sourcing everything except the feeds in-house. That is a great model to get *exactly* what you want to do everything you ask it to do.

However, the "build everything" model has the best fit explicitly because it is absolutely tailored to your mission activities, your network environment, and your organization. It will provide exactly the level of reporting you want, because you are deciding what it does, and how it works, and you are building the whole thing yourselves. Unfortunately, this level of detail and comprehensiveness does not come easily. It demands the highest cost of ownership. It is also the hardest, longest, and slowest to build out, launch, and get value from. In addition, do not forget that you will need both the skills, and the people to build the system and those to use and operate it. As noted above, those are usually two different groups of people at the very least, a fact that comes with its share of complications.

At the opposite end of the spectrum, you can look for off-the-shelf components, feeds, tools, and/or analyst support from a contractor, or a security, or intelligence shop to outsource everything. In the simplest form, you can say, "Here is the output I require, just send me the finished product, whatever that is, so that I can take some kind of action, or modify my posture or my business operations." They want the intelligence at the end of the production process from an outsourced provider, requiring them to build nothing at all themselves. This can be up and running very quickly. It neither requires that you hire nor have the necessary people or skills in-house. In addition, it lowers your cost of ownership. However, like anything bought off-the-shelf, you get what the market has, and it may not be everything you need.

The third option of course is to combine both ideas. Whatever options you are considering, it is imperative that you use *some* form of framework or rigorous construct to evaluate the pros, cons, and trad-eoffs. Herein, just as an example, we provide a simple matrix to look at various axes of evaluation for differing models, a useful framework since it goes beyond the technological architecture and ensures you also look at who is going to do the work as well.

HOW: Labor options or "How much do I do myself?"

Evaluating options of "build, buy, or hybrid" are best viewed in some framework to clarify the tradeoffs and priorities involved.

Axis of Evaluation	Build	Buy	Hybrid
Fit with mission	●		●
Supports the necessary activities	●	?	●
Can provide required metrics and reporting	●	●	●
Total cost of ownership	●		
Ease of implementation	●		
Speed to launch	●	●	
Availability of necessary skills (to build and staff)	?	●	?

◉ Cyveillance
a QinetiQ Company

The planning stage has got to include both architectural and technological framework, but should also consider how you plan to stand up this capability in terms of labor. You should ask the right questions – Do we build it? Do we buy it? Do we bring it in? Do we contract it? Do we contract it while we get up and running, and then either bring the contractors on board or let them go, and replace them with our own people? These are all things you have to think about because they will all affect your timeline, your project plan, and your budget. If you cannot answer these questions, you cannot make the effective budget requests, which may mean that they never get off the ground at all.

Whether you use this framework or another of your choice is far less important than ensuring you use *some* rigorous methodology for evaluating the options, tradeoffs, and advantages that each option – from "build it all" to "farm it out" to "somewhere in between" – will offer.

6.2 IMPLEMENTATION – THE BEST LAID PLANS

While talking with your peers during the planning process, you may encounter some who scratch their heads and say, "Gee, I do not even know if this whole thing is really justified." Some may know what to do and want to do it, but have no idea how. You are likely to find a small number who are already in their own planning phases or far beyond that, that is, in the build out phase. However far along you may or may not yet be, experience has shown that when implementation actually begins, there are some common landmines that tend to trip people up as they get going. Here is a very typical "speed bump" for example. Some people know what business objectives they want to accomplish. They have identified what mission activities they need to do operationally, as well as the types of data that they want to procure from various internal or external sources and vendors. In other words, they have got their "why" and their "what" pretty well sorted out. The thing they actually had not thought of is at the operational line level, or nuts and bolts, of how you plug these things into that thing over there. What is the box tool that you are going to get all of this stuff into to ensure the tool database platform's ability to support data? In some cases, the system's end users sign the subscriptions only to ingest them (and pay for them) for 6 months, and drop on the floor because they did not figure out ahead of time how to effectively manipulate or use the data, only to store it.

Another common sticking point is when groups start ingesting data feeds and spending money on them only to get stuck due to the dumbest of problems; the normalization of data. One user said that he did not realize for 45 days that the reason he and his team were not getting some of the correlations out of the engine they expected was because one vendor sent their offerings with a GMT timestamp whereas the others, all in California like the user, used Pacific-time-zone timestamps. The result was misalignment of data that prevented some important connections being made.

Similarly, "domain" and "host" are common fields in a wide variety of data feeds. But "host" does not always mean the same thing to every vendor. Some interpret "host" as synonymous with a second-level domain and a top-level domain, for example, domain.com. Other vendors provide it as www.domain.com, a problem because that is actually a host (www) within a domain (domain.com). Some would argue that "host" is actually synonymous with IP address, others point out that an IP can host many domains, each with many hostnames. On and on it goes, and if a process ends up affected as a result, the whole thing may grind to a halt. This normalization of disparate data sources is an extremely prosaic type of challenge, yet it is a sticking point that bunges up the works over and over again.

Another extremely common topic that was hinted at a little earlier is the question of skill sets. Do you have the know-how to both build the thing and run it? These two processes typically require two very different groups of people, so you definitely need to take this into consideration.

Finally, suppose everything is up and running. You are getting exactly the data that you need; you are transmogrifying it exactly the way you want, and you are actually getting good information out of the systems and people you have put in place. The question is: Do they actually know what to do when something bad happens? When the magic box and the team of geniuses discover that something has gone wrong, do they have the checklists, procedures, escalations, and phone trees to spring into action appropriately?

Going back to the definition of intelligence being actionable – if the professionals do not know what to do next and you have not thought through contingency plans or a "what to do" checklist ahead of time, then all the work up to that point is for naught. With a plan in hand, the organization will reap the benefits of all of the work that went into everything up to that moment. The experts have to know what to do when the unfortunate does occur. For example, do they unplug an infected machine from the network when they realize it is compromised? (An obvious choice, and one a nontechnical executive is almost sure to ask.) Or do they leave it running (despite the risk of data loss)? "Why in the world would you do that?" asks the executive. Answer: Because many sophisticated types of malware self-destruct when decoupled from the internet in order to frustrate forensic activities once they have been discovered. Unplug the box and you may lose all evidence of what happened or who is after you. There are many such thorny scenarios to think through – procedures, planning, and checklists are a critical component to ensure that once the capability is actually in operation, it delivers on its mission when the moment actually comes.

Who: Given Why, What, and How, Now You Can Ask Where To Get It

By this time in the process, you know – technologically and in terms of personnel – why you are doing it, what you are going to need, and how you plan to implement it. The next logical step from here is going out to the market and deciding whom to buy from. Now there are a lot of ways to compare vendors, but you should follow the pattern of looking first at the offering and then at the vendor themselves. For an offering, service, a source of data, a feed or intelligence, going for a pilot, or a trial will be helpful, but only if the client and vendor can agree on a framework for feedback and some concrete measures or axes of evaluation. If you intend to request service at no charge, a fair trade between buyer and supplier is the exchange of feedback for a brief period of service, and using an agreed framework for what defines "success."

WHO – Knowing WHY, WHAT and HOW, *now* ask where to get it

Once you know what intel you need to accomplish your goals, and how it will be implemented, how do you evaluate sources?

| Quality | Quantity* | Uniqueness | Timeliness | Value | Ease |

To effectively make the best choice, there are at least six axes on which customers or prospects should evaluate an intelligence or data vendor.

1. *Quality*: This is a tricky aspect because how it is measured varies from feed or data type to data type. Therefore, there must be some way to measure quality and you should agree on it before the trial.
2. *Quantity**: This one comes with an asterisk. Sometimes quantity is an indicator of value, since in many cases either more is better or less is better depending on the data in question. It is also quite possible that quantity is not actually applicable, since for example, you might have a feed that is extremely low volume, but even the occasional finding is of incredibly high value. For this element, you have to always look at the data type to understand whether volume is a valuable axis of comparison.
3. *Uniqueness*: Imagine if one vendor has good data but so do three other. If their offerings overlap by 85%, your decision has to be based on other factors as well. For example, you may get 85% of the same data from two vendors, but one guy may offer it 36 hours ahead of the other guy. If all other things are equal, in security, sooner is usually better, but if the data sets are different, uniqueness can be a key discriminator.
4. *Value*: When it comes to value, you may equate it to cost or it may have another axis of its own. If all vendors' offerings are functionally equal in every material respect, then lower price should win.
5. *Ease*: If one vendor's offering comes in a standard compliant JSON format that can be ingested with two scripts whereas another set is written in a proprietary flavor of XML which requires the efforts of two developers for a week, which one would you choose? Remember that effort costs time and money, so ease of implementation is a vital aspect of "value" to consider along with price.
6. *The vendors themselves*: So far we have mostly spoken about the product. You also have to look at the vendor. To be very candid, there are a lot of great things going on out there; a lot of neat technologies and many really cool companies doing really interesting things. However, if you are going to construct mission critical activities or risk mitigation plans around some of those

vendors, you need to be sure they are going to stick around. The great thing about small and new companies is they do great things. The bad thing is that four out of five of them fail very quickly. You need to have a look at the vendor's reputation, their customer base, their longevity, or their age in the industry.

WHO: Knowing WHY, WHAT, and HOW, *now* ask where to get it

In addition to the offering (i.e., the data, tool, feed, etc.), you must evaluate the provider, not just that which is provided.

| Reputation | Longevity | Stability | Security | Bench |

®Cyveillance

©Cyveillance, Inc. 2014   Cyveillance confidential

Invest your time in discovering the answers to important questions such as:

- Are they stable?
- Are they profitable? Running out of cash?
- What source of funding got them this far? Customers? Bootstrapping by the owners? Venture capital?
- Do they themselves have the kind of security you would expect from a security vendor?
- Are they audited?
- Do they have policies and procedures?
- Do they pen-test themselves?
- Have they ever been breached?
- If you need expertise skills or knowledge, how deep is their bench?

7.1 REPORTING AND MANAGEMENT COMMUNICATION

Finally, before concluding this book, a quick note about reporting and management communication is definitely needed. You have to communicate to management the value, the operational importance and the mission of what you are doing.

A lot of folks fall down when they start delivering reports around *nominal* metrics. In this case, they provide numbers around simple volume metrics, for example, the number of searches run, or the number of alerts that were triggered, or items investigated, or the number of documents that were found, tagged, discovered, or quarantined. The problem is that none of those translate directly to a mission outcome. Even if they do, you have to spell that out for management.

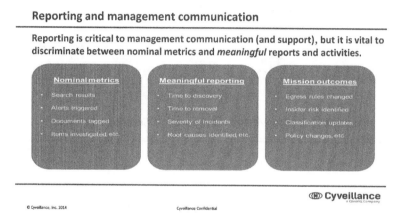

Reporting and management communication

Reporting is critical to management communication (and support), but it is vital to discriminate between nominal metrics and *meaningful* reports and activities.

Nominal metrics	Meaningful reporting	Mission outcomes
• Search results	• Time to discovery	• Egress rules changed
• Alerts triggered	• Time to removal	• Insider risk identified
• Documents tagged	• Severity of incidents	• Classification updates
• Items investigated, etc.	• Root causes identified, etc.	• Policy changes, etc.

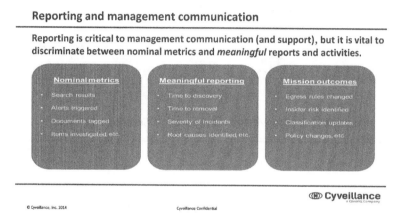

© Cyveillance, Inc. 2014   Cyveillance Confidential   ⟨⊕⟩ **Cyveillance** a QinetiQ Company

If those are nominal metrics, what are *meaningful* reports? Those would usually contain important data, such as:

- Time to discover an issue
- Time to remove the causes of a problem and remedy it
- The severity, not the number of incidents identified
- The number of root causes (which is important so that the nominal items do not keep growing or are reported)

Finally, *meaningful* metrics then have to translate to mission outcomes that can also be reported. For instance, if egress of sensitive data is uncovered, what actions ensue that can then be reported as concrete changes undertaken to reduce impact and future risk? If you identified an insider threat, did you change classification rules for data loss prevention (DLP) and egress monitoring? Have you instituted a policy change that should be communicated to the organization as a whole? Has HR been engaged or any personnel action taken? These are business outcomes that translate back to management of the business; nominal metrics alone will not make the leap to management communication effectively.

7.2 DEFINING AND ARTICULATING BUDGET NEEDS

Finally, if you know why you are doing it, what operational activities you will support, what intelligence needs you have, how you are going to implement it, and which vendors you want to buy it from (or at least what rough costs are for the tools and services you will need to buy), you are now ready to put together either an up-front or ongoing budget request.

If you are in the pre-operational stage, you will need to speak to the CFO to ask for both capex and opex. That is money to build the system and money to run it. To a CFO, those are two very different things. If these words or concepts are foreign to you, make sure to ask someone in finance or management to help you. If you only speak tech, and they only speak accounting, your budget request may face a rough road ahead.

Linking this concept back to the previous section, the managerial reporting you define will help dictate the program's long-term survival. Every budget cycle is bound to bring questions about the money spent and whether it is worth spending.

You have to be able to say, "Yes, we should still keep doing this and here is why." You should also be able to translate that back to the business. You need to make sure you have the right people to build and run a threat intelligence capability, and make clear what those people cost.

Another timely concern at this moment – you should know that given the current state of the market, those capabilities (in both building and operating a threat intelligence capability) are in great demand. To ensure that your operations do not get affected, consider looking at outsourcing, contractors, or training to improve the abilities of your own people, making an investment in them to help ensure that they stick around. For training, always choose the most loyal people, since the last thing you need halfway through the project is for someone to offer him or her a little more money, leaving you with a half-finished project and a newly created expert who just left for a competitor.

Last, but by no mean least, factor risk into your vendor evaluation. This is not only on the data side, but also on the provider. You have to evaluate the company, not just the offering, when ensuring the best and safest expenditure of your limited budget.

Conclusion and Recap

Throughout this book, we have covered a lot of ground, so a recap is always a good way to ensure that no idea has been left unexplored. When defining and building a cyber threat intelligence capability, it is always necessary that you ask these important questions:

- Why are you doing it? (Business objective)
- What do you need to do? (Activities in support of the Business objective)
- How are you going to implement it? (Architecture, operational model, etc.)
- Who will build it? Who will operate it? (Skills and sourcing options)

To end where we began, you must start with a clear business objective as it is the foundation stone of the whole project. It is what will bind and scope your "what" or your mission activities and the data or intelligence you need to support those activities.

In addition, you should avoid some of the predictable and known land mines where possible. However, always keep in mind that any implementation may require trade-offs in speed, fit, cost, and ease. Use some kind of matrix or rigorous model for this aspect, but remember to be rigorous about making your choices. They can have profound cost implications if you do not keep this in mind.

You must be able to turn those activities into metrics and reports that will matter to business management. If you cannot turn the data and mission activities back into operationally useful business outcomes and communicate them, you cannot succeed from a management standpoint even if you succeed from a security standpoint. Once you know what you are doing, how we are going to do it, and why you are doing it, only then should you worry about whom to go to buy something from. Before and during operations continue to define, and refine, how you will measure success, how you will communicate performance and activity, and prepare ahead of time for what to do when things go wrong.

If you start with "why," derive "what" you need. On the basis of that, establish "how" you will operate and then decide "who" to engage, you are well positioned to create, and successfully operate an effective threat-intelligence capability. Although these steps are not a guarantee of success, skipping them is almost assuredly a recipe for failure.

Printed and bound by CPI Group (UK) Ltd, Croydon, CR0 4YY

03/10/2024

01040424-0001

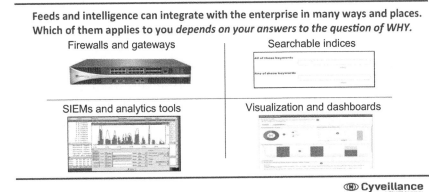